SANTIAGO CALATRAVA

SANTIAGO CALATRAVA

Liane Lefaivre
Alexander Tzonis

Motta Architettura

Santiago Calatrava

Cover
Faculty of Law Library, Zurich

Photo
Architekturphoto, Düsseldorf

minimum
essential architecture library

Series edited by Giovanni Leoni

Published Titles

Richard Meier
Pier Luigi Nervi
Álvaro Siza

For the excerpts reproduced in the sections
"Thought" and "Critique," the authors and publishers
wish to thank those who have authorised their
publication. The publisher is available for any queries
regarding sections for which it has not been possible
to trace the holder of the rights.

First edition: March 2009

ISBN: 978-88-6413-003-3

Printed in Italy

Contents

Portfolio

Introduction

Santiago Calatrava:
architect, engineer, artist, dream-worker

A decade before the end of the first millennium, the humanistic vision of unity of art and science in architecture seemed to be irrevocably lost. Technology and culture were understood as two uncompromisingly opposed forces. It is astonishing how fast the situation was reversed. Many people played a role in this development; without doubt one of the most important was Santiago Calatrava, architect, engineer, artist, and dream-worker. His building oeuvre and visionary projects manifest a genuine humanistic unity that combine rational intelligence with poetry; they restore enthusiasm for the art of construction, and most significantly demonstrate that utilitarian artifacts do not have to be oppressive and disruptive. They can evoke respect for their historical heritage even when they are inserted in landscapes of historical significance and built next to such as the Lusitania Bridge in Mérida, (1988-1991) and stir up a sense of community when constructed in urban centers as in the Hospital Bridges Murcia, Spain, (1993-1999). His designs often appear complicated and perplexing. The "strangeness" of their form is born out of a commitment not to follow the beaten track of reductive solutions and short term, frozen targets but to confront uncompromisingly multiple economic, technological, environmental, social, and cultural challenges. At the same time, his structures are intended to enable and inspire hope and to invite dreaming. Towards this end, essential design strategy is Calatrava's commitment to bring together structure and movement.

Structure and movement seem to be antithetical. Intuitively, most people assume that good structures are rigid not mobile and those which do not fulfil these conditions are associated with imminent danger and fear. No wonder designers of structures have routinely tried to express, emphasise and celebrate stability through *stasis*. But for structures, of course, movement is a basic fact of nature. From the vast "astral universe" to tiny plants and organisms, whose structure incorporates the gradual pace of their growth – to recall D'Arcy Thompson – their form resulting from movement responding to different load conditions, removing superfluous material and adding where and when needed.

In a similar way, in response to desires and aspirations, buildings are put together through movement, and it is through movement that they are taken apart at a certain point in time when their mission is over. While being used, buildings, as vessels and channels, are never at rest, movement being everywhere within their body, sustaining the flow of people and things. In addition, the more we understand the behavior of structures, the more we realize how, even if apparently immobile, they undiscernibly although perpetually move. While day and night, seasons, climatic conditions succeed each other, buildings slide and shudder, bend and bow, sway and tremble. Many designers have become involved with movement recently, but what distinguishes the contribution of Santiago Calatrava is that he expresses this reality in a unique way profoundly, intensely, and universally producing a coherent *poetics of movement*.

The most obvious way structures relate to movement is as containers accommodating the circulation of people or objects. This, by definition, is the case of infrastructure projects bridges and stations as well as buildings involving moving masses, projects that occupy a major part of Calatrava's oeuvre. Very early in his career Calatrava won a competition to design The Stadelhofen Station, a 270 meter-long train station in Zurich. It was immediately proclaimed a most successful integration of public transportation in an urban context and a natural setting. But it was also the outcome of Calatrava's capability to conceive it as a well formed organism made out of different interacting flows rather than a composition of static spaces. Within the complex the fast regular flow of trains along the tracks cutting through the ground level integrates with the hasty crowds entering and leaving the vehicles, approaching and leaving the station, ascending, descending, and walking through the shopping mall, under the tracks and over three steel bridges. However, Calatrava's achievement in creating a poetics of movement was in incorporating social as well as cultural aspects.

This achievement was due to his capability to cross-over from art, engineering and architecture

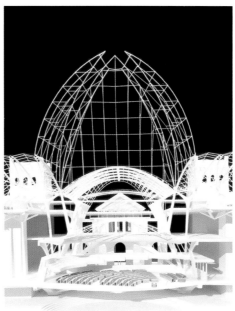

Reichstag model with
mobile covering, capable
of opening out like
a flower

opposite page
Hospital Bridge, Murcia

and back again, overcoming the abyss that
separates domains of knowledge today, but it was
also due to his capacity to link his innovative
explorations with a not so conspicuous but very
significant tradition in the history of design that
explored and exploited the relation between
movement and structures.

The connection between movement and structure
became an important issue in design, at certain
moments in history and in different parts of the
world besides Europe, such as Tibet and India.
However, the roots of Calatrava's poetics of
movement are probably to be found in a tradition
that draws from the vision of a "pillar of cloud"
swirling down from the sky and standing at the
tabernacle door in front of Moses in Exodus,
chapter 33 of the Bible, recalled in the spiral form
of the so called Salomonic Order column dear to
many late Renaissance painters. Examples of this
order are not rare in Spain, including the home
town of Calatrava, Valencia.

There is also the tradition of representation of
dynamic vegetal-organic, or flame-like objects to
be found during the Middle Ages, a notable
example being the famous building Lonja del
Mercado, also in Valencia, a building that much
impressed Santiago as a young boy, when visiting
the structure with his father. Clear echoes of this
can be easily found in the platform roof of the
Oriente Station in Lisbon.

Calatrava's explorations of movement in structures

Interior of the Faculty
of Law's library, Zurich
University

[1] Original title:
*On the Foldability
of Space Frames.*

engineering. Indeed, Calatrava's plural-disciplinary is founded on a series of systematic studies passing from one domain of knowledge to another. Thus, his early years as a student at the Art Academy in Valencia, in the mid-1960s, were succeeded by a period of studies in the Escuela Técnica Superior de Arquitectura, a relatively new institution, where he earned a degree in architecture and took a post-graduate course in city planning, and those by studies in civil engineering at the Federal Polytechnic University of Zurich, and finally years of academic research in the same institution investigating *The Foldability of Space Frames,* the subject of his Ph.D. dissertation. More precisely, his objective was to develop a method for transforming three-dimensional space frames into planar shapes and lines by moving their elements, that is certain types of movement in certain kinds of structures. The explicit usefulness of these studies is to be found in the long series of Calatrava's moving contraptions in buildings, which became one of the signature themes of his oeuvre, as in the dome for the Reichstag Conversion Competition in Berlin that was meant to open and close like a gigantic flower. The same with the opening of the Planetarium of the Science Center in Valencia, intended to shut and retract like the eyelids of a colossal, eerie cyclopic eye gazing into the sky, or the eye-shaped, moving roof in the library of the Zurich University, Law Faculty.

One of the most powerful effects of this theme is to be found in the garage doors of the Ernsting Warehouse and Distribution Centre in Coesfeld, Westfalen, – one of the very early works of Calatrava – wear functional requirements are combined with the dream-like surreal icon – when the door is lifted – of the slow movement of a bending knee, whose covering folds like clothing. The image of cloth waving in the wind is present on the "curtain wall" covering that hangs around the building. By felicitous coincidence, Ernsting is a textile firm which makes the blowing curtain effect even more suitable. Interestingly, the movement effect is emphasized by the contrast between the metallic material of the elements and their waving geometry that surrounds the building.

We find the same theme of fluttering movement of a fabric in the breeze in his so-called Plaza of the Nations on the Athens 2004 Olympic site, – echoing the flapping of the flags of the participating nations – now *actually* imbued with movement rather than just suggesting it through the geometry of the plane.

was also driven by the tradition of the "marvellous" machines, the *Mirabilia,* dating from Hellenistic times. With the "mechanization of the world picture" during the Middle Ages – from the 12th to the end of the 14th century – the tradition became important in Europe – as testified in the notebooks of the early engineers – and in the 17th and 18th century played a significant role in garden and outdoors architecture in the invention of "mobiles," "water structures," and pyrotechnics, while, finally, in the 20th century, it inspired the design of ludic toys for the enjoyment of children, such as those probably to be found among the toys of the child Calatrava.

However, Calatrava's "mirabilia," the parts of his buildings that move, are based on real, simple but at the same time ingenious mechanisms, the result of his academic investigations in mechanical

A more direct representation of movement, in fact of flying, is in the case of schemes where the structure takes the very shape of a bird's wing waving in the air as in the Lyon Airport Station, Satolas and the Tenerife Opera House which are configured imitating the silhouettes of flying birds. Such schemes work mentally by triggering associative memory, a very basic cognitive faculty, rather than reflection. Their impact is immediate and it leads to very widely appreciated popular projects. Even more effective, and dream-like, is when the structure that assumes the waving wing form actually moves, as in the Calatrava's first building in the United States – the expansion of the Milwaukee Art Museum, Milwaukee, Wisconsin, and the World Trade Center Transportation Hub in New York.

Increasingly, as the complexity of the Calatrava's projects grows and the sophistication of their technology advances, the work manifests a tendency to produce surrealist metaphors. To borrow a concept of Freud, Calatrava invites us to "dream-work," in an almost Bunuel-like way, to experience structures breaking free from the static world entering another kind of movement, that of generating possible worlds, of fulfilling a wish, of acting out a desire. Thus, concrete, categorized in the minds of most people as a hard and heavy material, is cast in the shape of the body of a dolphin and suddenly appears to strangely carry out the graceful movement or the hands of a dancer or the movement of the wings of a bird. Calatrava appears here using movement as the heir of the surrealist artists, movie directors and poets that Lewis Mumford once welcomed in New York as a necessary component of our machine civilization.

The folding frames of the space structures he studied are not only useful for conceiving the form of possible mobile containers. If we carefully observe the lines that make up his structures, as they fold, they trace circles, or other more complex curves, cycloids, epicycloids, cardioids, parabolas, or hyperbolas. They can be used, therefore, as mechanical devices called *linkages*, a kind of complex "compass" for generating new shapes and more intricate surfaces such as in many of his sculptures and especially the series of the Aegean Cycle, and certainly in the intricate geometry of the Auditorio de Tenerife, Santa Cruz, Canary Islands (2003), the two vaulted, open-air arcaded Agora, for the 2004 Athens Olympics running along the northern edge of the site to create a shady, curving

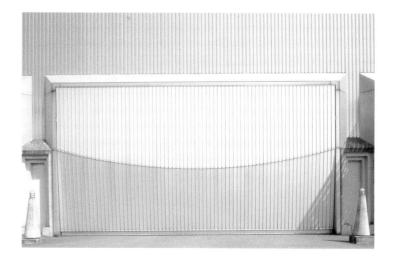

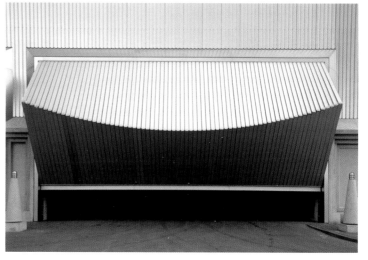

promenade, the Palau de les Arts Reina Sofía (2006) the most recent major building in Valencia's City of Arts and Sciences, and the airy roof of the Liège-Guillemins TGV Train Station.

The poetics of movement that Calatrava developed have taken the idea one step further of relating structure and movement, beyond the obsession with form, problem-solving, and simple surreal dream-working, into an inquiry seeking to define a moral system for human desire and action through metaphors of spatial-mechanical reasoning. Thus the poetics work as a framework for solving posed problems, explaining the complexity of those problems and, in addition, as in all cases of major cultural products opening avenues, for new inquiries for a better life.

Once more Calatrava worked his way, crossing-over from art, engineering and architecture and

Ernsting warehouse entrance

[2] The term, used by Alexander Tzonis, refers to groups of artworks, characterized by similarities to Minoan sculpture and, generally speaking, to Pre-Classical Aegean objects (editor's note).

The stadium and the Agora
at the Athens Olympic site

back again, as well as linking his innovative
explorations with a long term line of exploration in
the history of design that went into the relation
between movement and structures.

This time the roots of his approach go back to
antiquity, to the search to develop a conceptual
frame for representing the body in motion in
sculpture, at a time when Greek sculpture was
searching for ways of capturing dynamic aspects
of the world beyond the conventions of Egyptian
art. The ancient sculptor and writer Polyclitos is
accredited for establishing the fundamentals of a
component theory, in his book *The Canon*, written
in the 5th century B.C. But it was Quintilian, the
Roman theoretician of rhetoric and aesthetics,
who introduced the term *contrapposto,* to name
it. The literal meaning of the term is "counter
position." We do not know the exact content of
the essay by Polyclitos, which has been lost. But
later authors tell us that he prescribed the position
of the parts of the human body, according to his
own precepts. The body should be resting on one
leg, pushed a little to the rear, with the other leg

bent at the knee and applying less pressure. The
chest, while tilted backwards, should be slightly
bent, and the head should lean to the side in the
opposite direction to the chest. This "counter
posing" of the members of the body was seen as
expressing graceful movement, Polyclitos himself
practicing it in his own work.

Clearly, Polyclitos did not provide instructions for
depicting the image of specific, reallife moving
bodies. As indicated by the very concept of *The
Canon*, he created an abstract system of rules
based on axes and a set of relationships between
them. The abstract knowledge was drawn from the
body image but does not have to be
observational. It was a powerful framework able
to capture the most significant characteristics of
any kind of body in motion with the potential to
be applicable to any kind of structures.

We see the theory revived and revised by Giovanni
Paolo Lomazzo (1584). Lomazzo proposed the
figura serpentinata, or S-form as he called it,
because it resembled that letter. Lomazzo
accredited Michelangelo – who was planning to

write on the idea of movement – for originating the idea of the "serpentlike figure." Lomazzo's *contrapposto* and *figura serpentinata* were full of meanings and allusions about "the flame of fire" belonging to his time, the era of counterreformation.

One can easily recognise the figures of *contrapposto* and *figura serpentinata* in almost all the works of Calatrava as a signature figure: recall the supports at Stadelhofen Station, leaning to reach out, only to return; the Montjuic Communications Tower, and especially in his bridges. Calatrava's poetics, however, go beyond these figures as formulas to represent the moving body, or symbols in Lomazzo's iconology. He relates to them as abstract spatial schemata that capture the moment when a structure, as if arrested by an invisible power, is poised in a state of equilibrium and immobility, on the brink of imminent collapse whose meaning belongs to a discussion associated more with the major philosopher, writer, and moral thinker of the Enlightenment, Gotthold Ephraim Lessing, and his epoch-making book comparing art and poetry entitled *Laocoon*. Lessing went further in developing a theory explaining how immobile figures, in general, might imply movement. The paradigm he used was the newly discovered, much discussed sculpture in his time picturing Laocoon and his sons struggling as they are devoured by snakes, a seething mass of entwining serpentine lines and volumes.

Lessing's idea was that the artist, as opposed to the writer, "can use but a single moment of action…this single moment he makes as *fertile* as possible." The metaphor of fertility indicated a *non finito* process of generation – to use a category attributed to Michelangelo's sculptures in a state of partial benign incompleteness, the body or the face of a person barely emerging from the mass of the unworked material. It suggested the capability of a given figure in its present immobile state to recall a past and suggest a future state. In this single suspended moment, Lessing writes, the artist unites two distinct points of time, what has occurred before and what is to follow. Lessing's idea of the *contrapposto* and *figura serpentinata* was therefore cognitive.

We can recognize the "fertile moment" and its cognitive implications in Calatrava's single arch of the La Devesa Bridge in Ripoll, swerving on the point of collapse, soaring in its ascent, or in the mast of the Alamillo Bridge in Seville, its 40 meter-long pylon now "as-if" falling, now "as-though" rising. On the other hand, Calatrava's approach to movement goes beyond pictorial narrative aspects that preoccupied Lessing. He appears to join the aesthetic concept of the fertile moment with the engineering notion of the "critical point" – that is the point beyond which, if a certain variable in design is exceeded, the interatomic bonds of the material of the structure break and collapse. He appears to concentrate loads to a critical point, slimming sections to a critical extent, raising the slope lines to a critical degree and enjoying the results like an acrobat or even more like a shrewd dancer performing a physical feat. There is a deeper reward, however, here. We are led to recognize in the structure's shape, the diagram of operating forces. The diagram is vivid because of the articulated extremes of the seemingly contradictory form of the structure. Far from sublime, from arousing feelings of irrational fear, the effect of these critical conditions is cognitive. It allows two contrary readings simultaneously, like a Rubin diagram. The structure falls, then doesn't. Calatrava's structures might seem at this point contradictory appearing to aim at two opposite goals. The contradiction, however, is only a surface one. The paradoxes his structures violate are common sense beliefs, naïve intuitions, and banal expectations. They invite further thinking, broadening, deepening, and enriching our understanding of the world. They stimulate reflection and dream-work envisioning through oxymoron and paradox, ultimately leading to the search for an answer.

It is in this respect that the *poetics of movement*, central to Calatrava's creative process and his oeuvre, has an epistemological and moral meaning and for this reason they excite rather than offend, even when, using cutting edge technology, they stand conspicuously within nature, within densely populated urban historical settings, and when situated in socially challenging areas, environments in crisis, neighborhoods undergoing economic decline, or obsolescent industrial sites.

Chronology

1951	Santiago Calatrava Valls was born in Valencia
1968	Attends art school in Valencia (until1969)
1969	Studies architecture at the Escuela Técnica Superior de Arquitectura de Valencia, qualifies as an architect. Post-graduate Course in Urbanism
1975	Studies civil engineering at the Eidgenössische Technische Hochschule Zürich / Swiss Federal Institute of Technology (ETH Zurich), Zurich (until 1979) While at ETH, he produces a series of studies known as Alpine Bridges, which prefigure many of his future projects
1981	Doctorate in Technical Science at the Department of Architecture, ETH Zurich. Ph.D. dissertation: *On the Foldability of Spaceframes* Assistant professor at ETH at the Institute of Statistics, Construction, Aerodynamics and Light Structures in Zurich
1981	Opens an architecture and engineering studio in Zurich
1982	Becomes member of the International Association for Bridge and Structural Engineering (IABSE) in Zurich
1983	Stadelhofen Station in Zurich, his first large infrastructural project (completed in 1990) Ernsting warehouse in Coesfeld, Germany (completed in 1987) Lucerne station, Switzerland (completed in 1989)
1984	Bach de Roda-Felipe II Bridge in Barcelona (completed in 1987) Bärenmatte Civic Centre in Suhr, Switzerland (completed in 1988)
1985	"9 Sculptures by Santiago Calatrava" exhibit, Jamileh Weber Gallery, Zurich
1986	Concert hall for the San Gallo School of Music in San Gallo, Switzerland Tabouretti Theatre in Basel, Switzerland (completed in 1987)
1987	Auguste Perret Award, Union Internationale d'Architectes (UIA), Paris "Santiago Calatrava" exhibit, Schweizerisches Architetekturmuseum (SAM), Basel, Switzerland BCE Place: Gallery and Heritage Square, Toronto Alamillo Bridge and Cartuja viaduct, Seville (completed in 1992)
1988	Fazlur Rahman Khan International Fellowship for Architecture and Engineering at Skidmore Owings & Merrill, Chicago, Illinois Lusitania Bridge in Merida, Spain (completed in 1991) Emergency Service Centre in San Gallo, Switzerland (completed in 1991)
1989	Opens the Paris studio La Devesa Bridge in Ripoll, Spain (completed in 1991) Telecommunications tower in Montjuic, Barcelona (completed in 1992) Train station for the Lyon-St. Exupéry airport in France (completed in 1994) Faculty of Law library at the University of Zurich (completed in in 2004)
1990	Mèdaiile d'Argent de la recherché et de la Technique, Fondation Académie d'Architecture, Paris Campo Volantin Bridge in Bilbao (completed in 1997) Sondica airport in Bilbao (completed in 2000)
1991	Opens the studio in Valencia Kuwait Pavilion, Seville (completed in 1992) City of Art and Science, Valencia (completed in 2000) Tenerife Auditorium in Santa Cruz de Tenerife, Spain (completed in 2003)

| 1992 | Honorary member of the Real Academia de Bellas Artas de san carlos, Valencia
"Santiago Calatrava: Retrospective" itinerant exhibit at Netherlands Architecture Institute (NAI), Rotterdam
New parliament house for the German parliament in Reichstag, Berlin |
|---|---|
| 1993 | "Structure and Expression" exhibit, Museum of Modern Art (MoMA) in New York
Global Leader for Tomorrow World Economic Forum Award, Davos, Switzerland
East Station in Lisbon (completed in 1998) |
| 1994 | "Santiago Calatrava. The Dynamics of Equilibrium" exhibit at the Ma Gallery in Tokyo
Milwaukee Art Museum, Milwaukee (completed in 2001) |
| 1995 | "Santiago Calatrava: Construction and Movement," Fondazione Angelo Masieri, Venice |
| 1996 | "Santiago Calatrava: Opere e progetti 1980-1996" Exhibition, Palazzo della Ragione, Padova, Italy
"Santiago Calatrava" exhibit at the Milwaukee Art Museum, Milwaukee
Bridge of Europe, Orléans (completed in 2000)
Valencia opera House, Valencia (completed in 2006)
TGV Liège-Guillemins train station, Liège, Belgium |
| 1997 | *Doctor of Science Honoris Causa*, Technische Universiteit Delft/Delft University of Technology, Delft, Netherlands
"Santiago Calatrava: Structures and Movement" exhibit, National Museum of Science, Technology and Space, Haifa, Israel
Louis Vuitton Art Award – Moet Hennessey, Paris
Structural Engineering Certificate from the State of Illinois Department of Professional Engineering in Springfield, Ilinois
Temporary permit to practice structural engineering from the State of California in Sacramento |
| 1998 | Officer of the Order of Arts and Literature (l'Ordre des Arts et Lettres), Republic of France, Paris
Guest Lecturer, School of Architecture and Design, Massachusetts Institute of Technology, Cambridge. Massachusetts
Cantine Isios, San Sebastiàn, Spain (completed in 2001)
Puente de la Mujer, Buenos Aires (competed in 2001)
Petah-Tivka Bridge in Tel Aviv (completed in 2003) |
| 1999 | Príncipe de Asturias de las Artes Award, Fundación Príncipe de Asturias, Spain
The New York Times Time Capsule, sculpture commissioned by the *New York Times*, New York
Hoofvaart Bridges, Netherlands (completed in 2004) |
| 2000 | *Doctor Honoris Causa of Architecture*, Università degli Studi di Ferrara, Ferrara, Italy
Guest Lecturer at the School of Architecture and Design, Massachusetts Institute of Technology, Cambridge, Massachusetts
"Santiago Calatrava: Scultore, Ingegnere, Architetto" exhibit, Palazzo Strozzi, Florence
Honorary Academician, Real Academia de Bellas Artes de San Fernando, Madrid |
| 2001 | "Calatrava: Poetics of Movement" exhibit, Meadows Museum, Southern Methodist University, Dallas, Texas
"Santiago Calatrava: Esculturas y Dibujos" exhibit, IVAM Centre Julio González, Valencia
Sports complex for the Olympic Games in Athens (completed in 2004)
Katehaki Bridge, Athens (completed 2004)
Neratziotissa train and underground station, Athens (completed in 2004) |
| 2002 | Best of 2001 Award for the Milwaukee Art Museum, *Time Magazine*, New York, NY, USA
Il Principe e L'Architetto Award for the design of the bridge on the canal Grande in Venice, awarded in Bologna |

Sir Misha Blackl Award, Royal College of Art, London
Leonardo da Vinci medal , Société Européenne de Formations des Ingènieurs (SEFI), Brussels
Bridge for light rail transport, Jerusalem (completed in 2008)
80th South Street Tower, New York (work in progress)

2003   Medalla al Mérito a las Bellas Artes (medal), Real Academia de San Carlos
de Valencia, Valencia
"Santiago Calatrava: Wie ein Vogel/Like a Bird" exhibit, Kunsthistorisches
Museum Wien, Vienna
Grande Médaille d'Or, Architecture (gold medal), Académie D'Architecture, Paris

2004   Opens studio in New York
"World Trade Center Transportation Hub" exhibit, Museum of Modern Art (MoMA), New York
Doctor Scientiarium Honoris Causa, Technion-Israel Institute of Technology, Haifa, Israel
Valencia towers (work in progress)
Permanent transportation centre at the World Trade Centre in New York (work in progress)
2004 Gold Medal, Queen Sofia Spanish Institute, New York

2005   AIA Gold Medal, American Institute of Architects, Washington
Eugene McDermott Award in the Arts, Council for the Arts, Massachusetts Institute
of Technology, Cambridge, Massachusetts
Time 100, *Time Magazine*, New York
"Sculpture into Architecture" exhibit, Metropolitan Museum of Art, New York
"Clay and Paint: Ceramics and Watercolors by Santiago Calatrava" exhibit at the Queen
Sofia Spanish Institute, New York
Chicago tower (work in progress)
Città dello Sport and Faculty of Law and rectorate in Tor Vergata, Rome (work in progress)
Fordham Spire in Chicago, Illinois

2006   Premio Nacional de Ingeniería Civil 2005, Ministerio de Fomento, Madrid

2007   "Santiago Calatrava: Escultures, dibuixos i ceràmiques " exhibit, Es Baluard Museu d'Art
Modern i Contemporani de Palma, Palma de Mallorca, Spain
Premio Nacional de Arquitectura 2005, Ministerio de Fomento, Madrid
Doctor of Arts, *Honoris Causa*, Columbia University, New York, NY, USA
"Santiago Calatrava: Dalle forme all'architettura " exhibit, Scuderie del Quirinale, Rome
Tanner Lectures at Yale University, New Haven

2008   *Doctor Philosophiae, Honoris Causa* from Tel Aviv University, Tel Aviv
Lecturer on "Becoming an Architect" at Azrieli School of Architecture, Tel Aviv
Included in the Gran Cruz de la Orden de Jaume I from the Municipality of Valencia

Works

Stadelhofen Railway Station
Zurich, Switzerland, 1983-1990

General ground plan

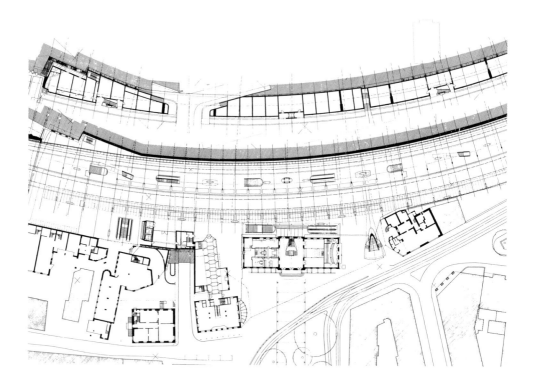

The Stadelhofen Railway Station is located in a dense urban area at the foot of a steep hill, once part of a bastion of Zurich's ancient fortifications. Besides building new platforms, the project included, on one hand, connecting the upper and lower levels of the town with pedestrian bridges and, on the other, providing an underground shopping center. Calatrava's section drawings show a highly complex, multi-level pedestrian traffic system. One series of stairwells and escalators on the platforms leads to pedestrian bridges over the tracks to the other side while another series leads to the underground shopping area under the tracks. Aside from its optimal functionality, the project is exceptionally enjoyable and captivating.

On the higher level, for example, two arched pedestrian bridges lead to what Calatrava has transformed into a gently winding promenade. Flanking the hillside and extending lengthwise along the station, covered by a leafy pergola, it creates a

charming passage to the upper town, also
serving as a protective covering for the train
platform at ground level. Again on ground
level, the waiting passengers on the opposite
side of the tracks are protected by a
cantilevered glass roof system in which
winged columns hoist up a torsion tube
attached to steel flange purloins.
As for the underground shopping area, it
hardly feels subterranean. The exposed
concrete ceiling and walls form a continuous,
gently curved surface, through which natural

daylight filters via prefabricated glass-block
elements in the platforms, creating an airy
luminescence for the shopping street.
The railway station has proven a success
as has the recreation of the park across
the street.
A pole of attraction that offers cafés
and restaurants, the project has magnetized
what Baudelaire referred to as *flaneurs*,
citizens out for a leisurely, hedonistic
urban stroll in the midst of a modern,
bustling city.

Platforms seen from
crossing walkways

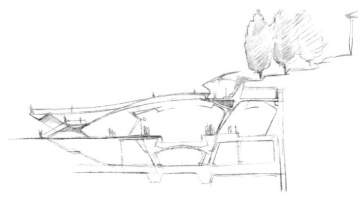

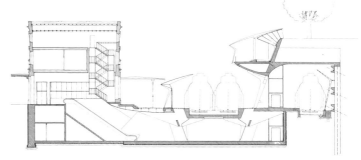

above
The platform and tracks
next to the hill,
on the opposite side
of the station

below
Transversal sections
of the station

opposite page
Underground floor
and lighting system

Alamillo Bridge
Seville, Spain, 1987-1992

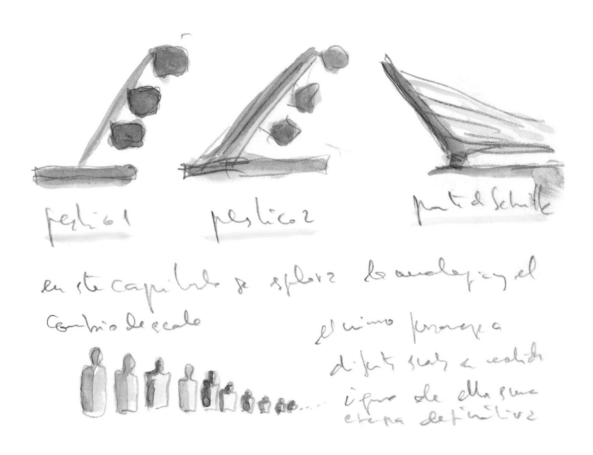

Early studies for the bridge, watercolors from the architect's notebook

When in 1992 Seville became the site of the World's Fair, the city took advantage of the opportunity to improve its infrastructure and that of the surrounding areas in the province of Andalusia. For Calatrava it became a concrete opportunity to develop his vision of infrastructure as a cultural object and of bridges as works of art. Spanning 200 metres over a section of the Guadalquivir River, the bridge is connected to a viaduct for automobiles, cyclists, and pedestrians. The site is unusual in that the same river has two crossing points located in close proximity to each other. In response to this setting, Calatrava initially proposed two bridges featuring a pair of asymmetrical, 142-metre-high pylons positioned at an angle of 58 degrees – following the same slope as the pyramid of Cheops, as Calatrava points out – to span the two sections of the river. The identical bridges, with their pylons tilted toward each other, would have formed a huge

triangular space, akin to the side of that same pyramid, its apex high in the sky. But the idea was not accepted and only one bridge was built. Calatrava has called the bridge "heroic." Indeed it triumphs over common sense notions about how structures stand. It was a new type of cable-stayed bridge, where the weight of the pylon was sufficient to counterbalance the deck. Instead of backstays, thirteen pairs of stay cables from the single pylon support the bridge.

The construction process added to the bridge's uniqueness. The pylon and platform were constructed by lifting segments of the steel shells of both into place with a large, high-capacity crane, tying them together with their respective stay cables and then filling them with reinforced concrete. Completed in thirty-one months, the bridge not only improved the regional infrastructure between Seville and its neighbouring towns, but created a monument emblematic of the region's booming dynamism.

Aerial view of the bridge and the Guadalquivir River

following pages
Front views of bridge

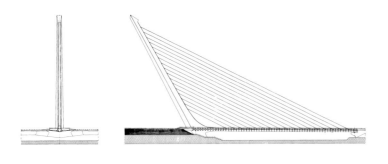

City of Arts and Sciences
Valencia, Spain, 1991-1996

Aerial view of complex

It takes a non-conformist visionary to design an observatory in the form of an eye. This is what Calatrava did when, in 1991, he received the commission to develop a whole complex, located on the dry bed of the Turia River, which was to be called the City of Arts and Sciences. It now houses a planetarium, a science museum and an opera house. Containing an IMAX theatre, the architectural "eye" of the planetarium has an "eyelid" that opens to permit access to the surrounding shallow pool. The planetarium is made up of a gigantic concrete half-sphere under a transparent concrete shell 110 metres long and 55.5 metres wide, which forms the "eyelid" over the half sphere that incorporates a system of slats mounted on each side of pivoting central stems. As the mobile parts of the structure open out, they reveal the dome,

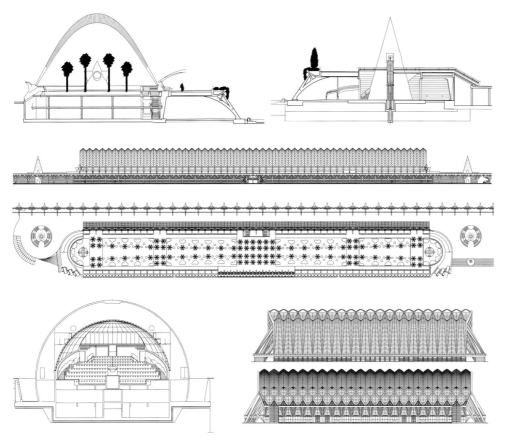

from above
Transversal sections, front views, ground floor plan of the Science Museum, section of the planetarium and front views of the museum

page 44
above
Early draft drawings of the planetarium
below
View of the Science Museum

page 45
Partial view of planetarium's eye-shaped element

giving it an appearance of lightness. The shallow, mirror-like pool reflects the building above in order to create the illusion that the eye is whole. The pool, set on a glass bottom, acts as a translucent roof of the library, auditorium, and restaurant facilities bathed with day light from above.
Next to the eye-shaped building is the Science Museum. It has the no less unusual form of a splashing wave – perhaps a reference to the Turia River in whose now dry bed the building rises. With its metal and glass structure, it resembles Paxton's Crystal Palace and other grand exhibition pavilions of the past, only its shape is meant to convey dynamism and asymmetry rather than stability and order. It is a constructional tour de force, employing as it does the same curving module five times along the length of its site development of transverse sections.

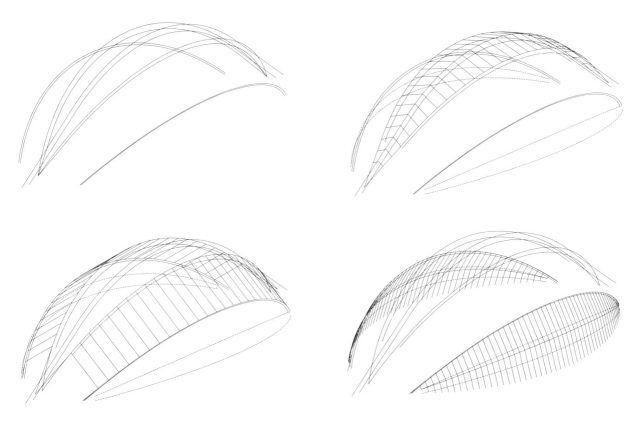

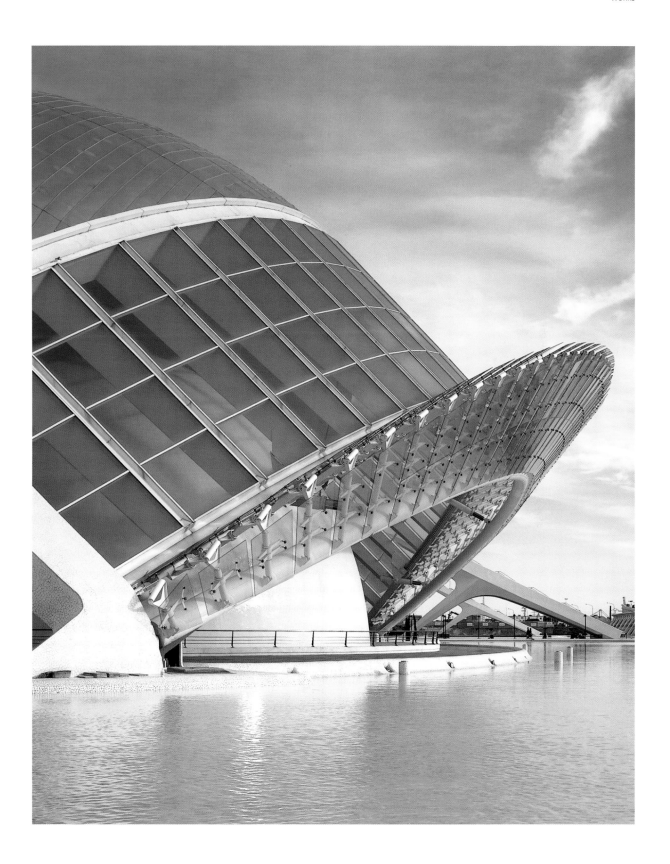

Alcoy Community Hall
Alcoy, Spain, 1992-1995

Passageway under the
square

opposite page
General ground plan

page 48
above
West end of square
with semi-open,
east end entrance
below
Drawings showing
the mechanism
for the entrance's
movement and its east
end open

page 49
The east end closed

In 1992 Calatrava was commissioned the remodeling of Plaza de España, the central square in the Valencian town of Alcoy, a venue of powerful historic worth, traditionally associated with festivals and community events. The commission also included the construction of the Alcoy Community Hall to complement the Church of Santa Maria and the town hall as a subterranean multipurpose public space for cultural and social events.

The subterranean hall is entered at either end of the plaza. The western entrance is set below grade and protected by a stainless steel, pentagonal grid of slats, which become part of the plaza surface when closed. When raised, the suspended door structure leads the eye to the entrance and the stairs leading underground. At the east end of the plaza, by the church, the entrance is paradoxically marked by a circular pool. The pool features a mechanical cover composed of a metal grid that can be closed to form a secure surface for pedestrians. The entrance here leads down beneath the basin of the pool and into the hall.

The primary support structure of the roof of the underground hall is a system of concrete arches which create a passageway along a longitudinal axis.

The resulting awe-inspiring geometry can be likened to the unfolding space of a medieval gothic building. But the imagery of entering the underground through a body of water and entering an arched ribbed structure also intentionally alludes to entering the stomach of Jonah's whale.

As for the piazza, a series of translucent glass panels mounted in stainless steel frames inserted between the arches of the hall below filter daylight into the hall. At night, the reverse occurs. A gentle light emanates from below, turning it into a mysteriously glowing surface.

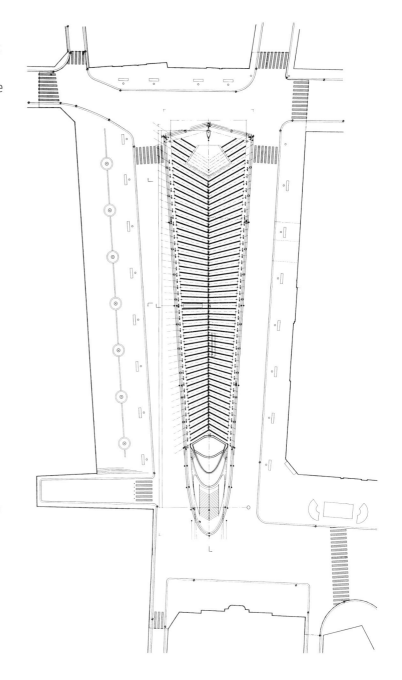

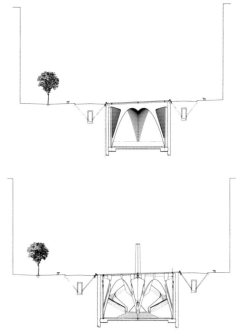

Milwaukee Art Museum
Milwaukee, Wisconsin, Usa, 1994-2001

Ground plan

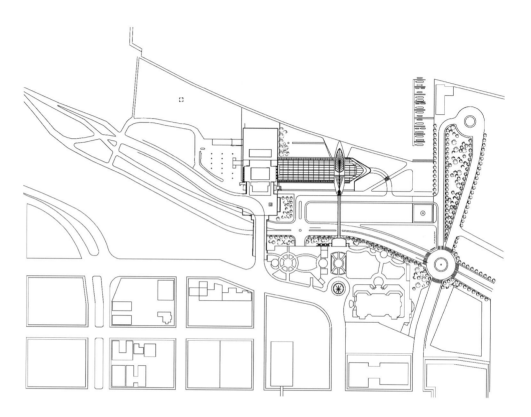

The original building complex consisted in a rectangular concrete structure, connected to the city by a concrete bridge. Due to the growing importance of the museum, research was carried out to seek out a stronger architectural identity with a tender called. The competition brief stipulated a new grand entrance, which was to serve a point of orientation for visitors, as well as a whole new architectural identity for the entire structure. Needless to say, Calatrava's design more than filled the bill.

Dramatically perched on the axis of Milwaukee's main street, the bird-like building has a *brise soleil* in the form of two wings. Reaching a breadth of 217 feet at its highest point, the 90-ton structure is wider than a Boeing 747-400 airplane. Weather permitting, these "wings" open daily when the Museum itself opens and close when it closes; they gracefully open and close once a day exactly at noon, like a colossal wild white swan about to take flight.

The Milwaukee Art Museum had been

partially housed in a building designed in 1957 by Eero Saarinen as a war memorial. From the outset, two lower floors were allocated for use as an art gallery. Further exhibition space was created in 1975 by David Kahler's addition, a structure that serves as a plinth for the Saarinen building. Calatrava proposed this white steel and concrete pavilion, which contrasted sharply with the existing buildings. It linked directly to Wisconsin Avenue via a cable-stay footbridge supported by a mast inclined at a 47 degree angle, parallel to the pivot line of the *brise soleil*. The interior is also spectacular. Calatrava's design almost doubled the original 14,900 square metres of the museum, adding: a linear wing that is set at a right angle to Saarinen's structure and housing a new atrium; 1,500 square metres of gallery space for temporary exhibitions; an education centre with a 300-seat reading room; a gift shop; and a 100-seat restaurant, which is positioned at the focal point of the pavilion and commands a panoramic view over the lake.

Building's profile with wings open

following pages
Photo taken with high exposure time, where the various stages of the wings' movement, can be seen; overall view of the building

51

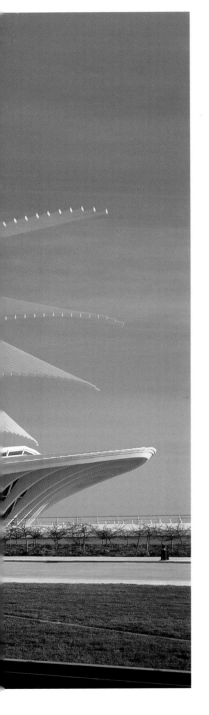

Centro de Arte Reina Sofía
City of Arts and Sciences, Valencia, Spain, 1991-2004

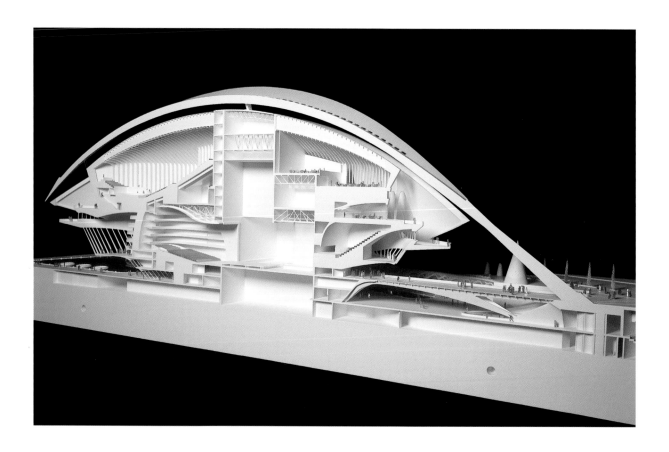

Transversal section model
of the complex

Perhaps it is the fact that we hear the most haunting music inside our own heads that inspired Calatrava to design this head-shaped opera house. Whatever the case, the head-like building, made up of two symmetrical, cut-away concrete shells, rises next to the Science Museum in the shape of a wave and next to the Planetarium in the shape of an eye in this surreal cluster of buildings by Calatrava in the City of Arts and Sciences in Valencia.
Conceived as the final element in the City of

Arts and Sciences complex, the Centro de Arte Reina Sofía consists of a complex of auditoria for music and drama, halls and vestibules for social events that accompany the performances, and facilities that sustain their function. Access to the building is by means of a 53 metre-long gangway up in the air on the western side. Two symmetrical side corridors guide people from the main access into a foyer leading to the opera house.
The Main Hall occupies the centre of the

complex and can seat 1700 people; it is set within an acoustically shaped shell embedded within the central core together with its scenery facilities and lifting mechanisms for the stage and orchestra pit.

A smaller auditorium, conceived mainly for chamber music, seats 400, while a large open-air auditorium to the east, protected partially by the open shell, can seat 2,000 for plays and other performances, offering spectacular views of the complex as well as the possibility of viewing performances on special video screens.

Further events can be staged at various locations set amongst its various spaces. For the open-air performance areas, the roof and defining walls enclosing the complex serve an acoustic function, while a glass-covered, insulated rehearsal area is provided above the chamber music hall. All auditoria are equipped with the cutting edge technology nowadays required to produce music or drama.

Façade of the Reina Sofía behind the planetarium

page 56
Partial view of the Reina Sofía

page 57
One of the many external spaces used as a panoramic terrace overlooking the city landscape

Ysios Winery
Laguardia, Spain, 1998-2001

Interior view

Starkly simple, this work reveals Calatrava's remarkable sensitivity to the natural landscape. Located in the Rioja wine-growing region of Spain, about an hour south of Bilbao by car, the Ysios winery is one of the first wineries in Spain to have adapted the French practice of the *grand cru*.

The winery is sited in such a way that it stands out against the blue mountain range of the high sierras of the Pyrenees. The roof, made of aluminium-clad cypress beams, rides like a gentle wave over the land, accentuated by the mirroring pool of water which encircles the base of the building. Rather than bearing down on the land, it derives its buoyant, rippling forms from the topography in which it is nested.

The ripples are not there for just an aesthetic effect. The sinusoidal wooden walls, for all their thinness, are extraordinarily strong. A flat

wall of the same thickness would not have been capable of bearing the load of the 36 gigantic stainless steel barrels big enough to hold the 25,000 litres of wine nor the 1,000,000 tons of grapes that the building routinely handles. These gracefully rippling curves in fact constitute the most robust structure possible. Calatrava's geometry, like his predecessor Antoni Gaudi's, is the result of an extremely rigorous constructional logic. It is

not there to complicate the building but to simplify it. As a result, it seems to be in harmony with the laws of nature.

This is not just a dramatic building to be looked at from the outside. Calatrava has ensured it is also a building to look out from. With its swooping pinnacle crowning a ten-metre high curved picture window, it provides a panoramic view of the bucolic countryside and of the small hilltop town of Laguardia in the distance.

Building's wavy profile, in each season, becoming a part of the context's topography

page 60
above
Front of the building
below
Longitudinal section and ground floor plan

page 61
Curvilinear layout of the covering

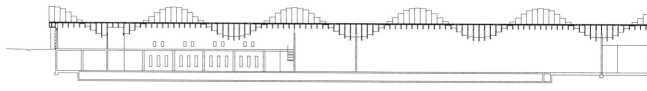

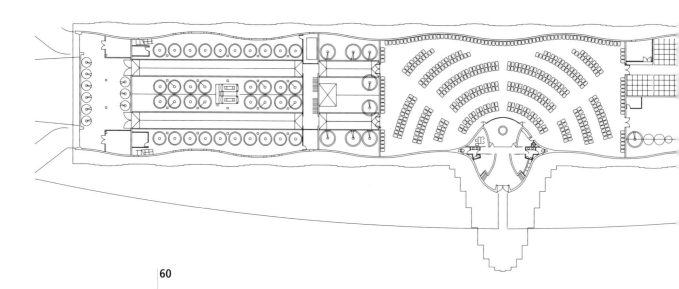

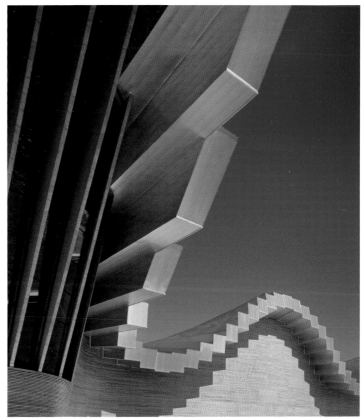

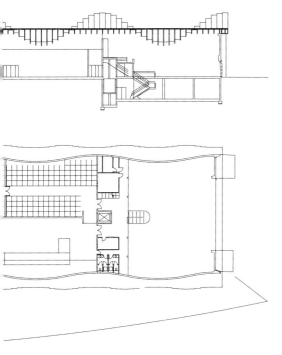

Puente de la Mujer
Buenos Aires, Argentina, 1998-2001

View of bridge and port

There is a particularly difficult though agile tango movement in which the woman rests her weight on one bent leg, using it as a pivot while she swings the other leg on the floor in a circle with her back inclined backwards towards the outstretched leg. There is a reminiscence of this movement in the suspenseful and tense movement of the Puente de la Mujer when its mobile section swivels on its axe to let passing ships through.

In 1998 Calatrava was asked to design a bridge intended to mark the renewal of the surrounding areas of Puerto Madero, the old harbor of Buenos Aires, similar to those areas where the tango was born.
He proposed a single inclined pylon. The pylon is 39 metres high, from which a rotating 102-metre deck is suspended by cables and set between a pair of fixed bridges.
The rotating section can turn 90 degrees to

allow free passage of water traffic. The weight of the mechanical tower balances the weight of the pylon. The total bridge length is 160 metres. The material for the structure is reinforced concrete and steel while ceramic and natural stone were used for the paving. At night special lighting emphasizes the urban civic character of the area, which was redeveloped into a commercial, residential, and tourist district.

In addition to its symbolic role, the bridge was expected to improve pedestrian routes until then inadequately connected to the urban fabric, as well as to the nearby axis created by the town hall, the Plaza de Mayo, and the Plaza Rosada.
The footbridge for a dock still used for water traffic enhances pedestrian circulation and connects the plazas on either side of the embankment.

page 64
above
Aerial view of the bridge with city in the background
below
Drawings with the bridge's profile, when open and closed

page 65
High exposure time image, where the inclined pylon's movement can be seen

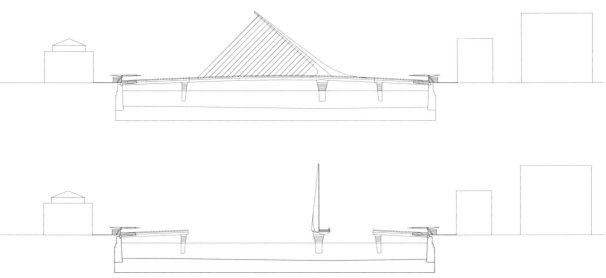

Bridges over the Hoofdvaart
Hoofddorp, Netherlands, 1999-2004

View of row of three
bridges: Harp (to the front),
Lyre and Lute

opposite page
The Lyre

A harp, a lyre and a lute. When asked, by the regional government, to design three bridges over the Hoofvaart canal to the west of Amsterdam's Schipol Airport by the regional government as part of its infrastructure planning, this is the imagery Calatrava conjured up. Each bridge is, symbolically, one of these string instruments.

The three bridges were designed to be read both as individual markers identifying their particular locations and as an ensemble defining the area of Hoofddorp as a whole. Indeed, given the flatness of the polder landscape, pedestrians, cyclists, drivers, and even airline passengers while landing at the nearby airport can view all three bridges at once from a certain distance. This is a typical characteristic of many parts of the Dutch landscape where the sea was initially drained and the area claimed for agriculture and then later turned into what are how housing, leisure and business accommodations.

Each of the bridges is a variation on the theme of the inclined cable-stayed steel pylon structure in the form of a spindle, and they all seem to be dancing a playful, rhythmical, musical gigue. The first bridge in this sequence is the harp, which features the largest pylon of the three bridges, with a height of 73 metres and a total length of

142.83 metres (with two spans of 86.94 and 55.89 metres). The Lyre is situated on the other side of this projected green area, providing access to the town of Hoofddorp. It consists of two connected spans, a lower bridge 19.6 metres long and a flyover set perpendicular to it with a total length of 148.8 metres composed of two spans 74.4 metres long whose cables are ingeniously linked to the pylon, which rises to a height of 58 metres. In the harp, on the contrary, the pylon's inclination shares the same plane as the stays. The vertical curvature of the deck expresses faithfully and elegantly the forces at play.

side
The Lute

below
The Lyre

opposite page
The Harp

Quarto Ponte sul Canal Grande
Venice, Italy, 1999-2008

The new structure's curved
profile in its context

opposite page
Plan

The construction of a new pedestrian bridge over the Grand Canal, only the fourth to be built since the 16th century, is of considerable importance. The canal was first spanned by the Rialto Bridge, built between 1588 and 1591. The Accademia Bridge was added in 1932 (and rebuilt in 1984), and the Scalzi Bridge was constructed in 1934. In 1999, the Municipality of Venice drafted a preliminary plan for a fourth bridge and Santiago Calatrava was commissioned to design it. The project is sited at the point connecting the railway station (at the north end of the bridge) with the Piazzale Roma to the south. It is therefore important both functionally and symbolically, giving visitors their first impressions of Venice and providing a panoramic view of the Grand Canal. The sleek, low profile of the Quarto Ponte sul Canal Grande is an exercise in euphemistic, minimalist understatement. Care has been taken to integrate the bridge with the quays on either side. The stepped areas at

either end act as extensions of the bridge, creating new public spaces for Venice. The steps and deck of the bridge are made of alternating sections of tempered security glass and natural Istria stone, picking up the design of the existing paving. The abutments, made of reinforced concrete, are clad in the same stone. At night, thin line of fluorescent bulbs set within the handrail only enhance the serenely simple line of the bridge, also illuminated from below its transparent deck.

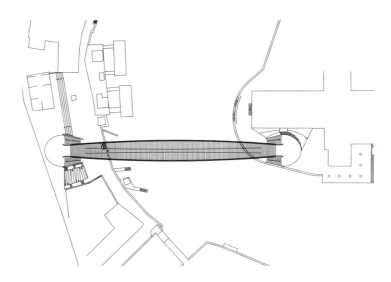

Points of the structure's
ground anchorage

opposite page
View of the bridge

Olympic Site
Athens, Greece, 2001-2004

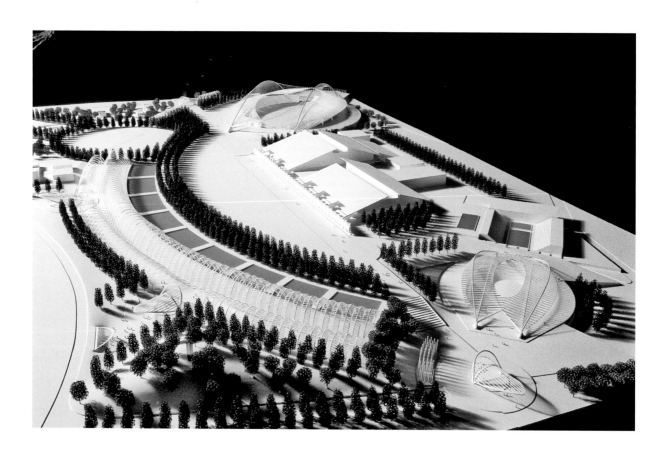

Model of the Olympic complex

In October 2001, just les than three years before the Games were to take place, Calatrava officially received the commission from city officials and the organizing committee to design all the elements of the Athens Olympic Sports Complex as well as its master plan. His major concern was the overall quality of the area within which his buildings were to be inserted.

He proposed a rigorous spatial reorganization of the site to serve athletes, the public, and the news media, as well as a permanent centre for athletic and cultural events with an upgraded transportation system within an ecologically sustainable, park-like setting replete with olive trees and cypresses. He also conceived a new roof for the Olympic Stadium, a complete refurbishing of the Velodrome, various entrance plazas and entrance canopies for the complex, and a central Plaza of the Nations with tree-lined boulevards and a sculptural, so called Wall of

Nations. Along each side of the stadium, aligned with the longitudinal axis, cable-braced, curving cantilevers hang on central tubular arches forming two spherical segments covered by stretched fabric. During the Olympics, these roof canopies anchored to pivot-points in the elevated plinth were meant to shade the open stands and define the silhouette of the structure.

The Plaza of the Nations, a monumental white tubular steel wall sculpture, occupies a sloping, semicircular area at the heart of the complex, between the northern Agora and the central circulation spine. It can be used as a backdrop for shows and theatrical productions. It can also be used as a screen for announcing events on the giant video display on the Wall of Nations.

Or it can be animated to simply flutter freely against the sky in a world of its own, high above the fiercely competitive activities of the Olympics below.

above
The Agora's arches

side
The Wall of Nations
in motion

opposite page
left
The Olympic torch
right
Detail of the curvilinear
Wall of Nations

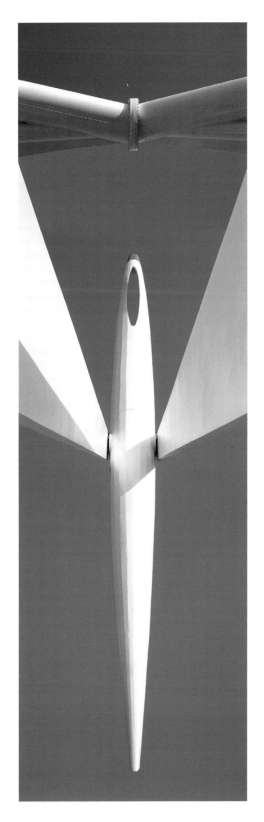

Light Railway Train Bridge
Jerusalem, Israel, 2002-2008

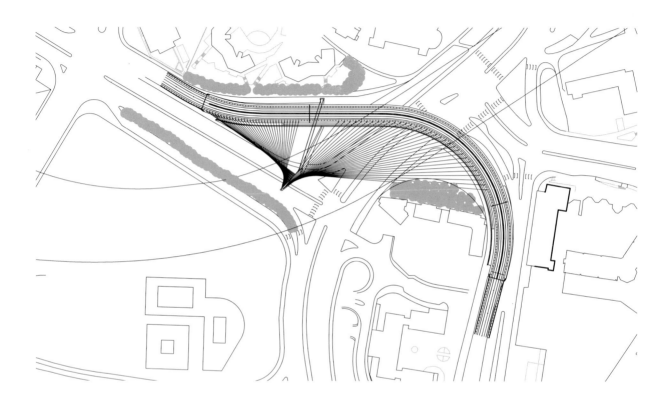

General ground plan

The city of Jerusalem, Israel, intending to enhance its transportation services, decided to introduce a light railway train system to connect various parts of the city and its environs. Located on a transportation hub at the intersection of the ancient Jaffa Road, the new Tel Aviv Highway and Herzl boulevard leading to Yad Vashem Holocaust Museum, it was considered from the outset not only as an infrastructure project but also as a landmark structure that would function as a modern gateway to the city while maintaining continuity with the past.

The site lacked distinction. In addition to a master plan for the site, the proposal also included several alternative bridge schemes — an arch bridge and cable-stayed bridge, each with inclined, straight, or curved pylons — and a proposal for the rehabilitation of the site's immediate conditions. Calatrava also

considered the impact of the structure on the existing urban context and on the future development of the area. The idea of a cable bridge, being the least intrusive, dominated the proposal process and was ultimately adopted with an inclined pylon and a bridge deck with a curved alignment. The pylon of the bridge stands like a huge flame blown by the desert wind, to borrow an image from Yehuda Amichai's *Jerusalem*, or, like a huge tilting

mast, announcing Jerusalem as "a port on the shore of eternity," or the "Venice of God." Despite the apparent newness of his bridges inside a historical milieu, Calatrava's approach does not negate memory. What he refuses is a passive and amnesiac attitude toward the past and its objects, events, and actions. Within a landscape heavy with the conflicting forces of history, the bridge suggests the potential of intelligence, creativity, and dialogue.

Converging point of various fast roads in a bordering area of Jerusalem's historical centre

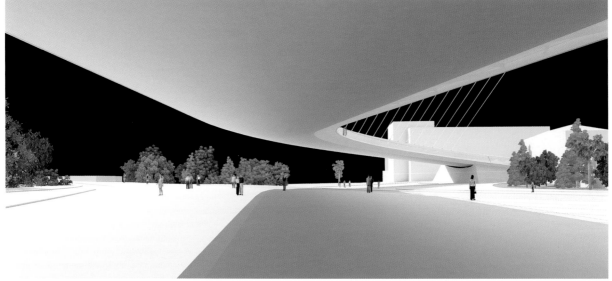

The pylon's peak,
bent over and inclined,
with a masterful use
of cables

opposite page
Models

Projects

Permanent World Trade Center
New York, USA, 2004

The forceful, revitalizing phoenix-like symbolism of the winged structure for the Battery Park area of the new World Trade Center was unveiled in 2004, in the aftermath of 9/11. It proved to be immensely popular with the New York public, still traumatized by the tragic events of 2001.

Filled with hope and vitality, the structure returns to New York what the September 11 tragedy has taken away. It also brings back an element that New York had lost: the commitment to large-scale, public urban and infrastructure projects that serve and celebrate the community in the manner that the Brooklyn Bridge, Central Park, Pennsylvania Station, and Grand Central Terminal once did.

One could say that Calatrava is a master at employing not only glass, steel, concrete, and stone but also light as a construction material. The bird-like structure and surrounding translucent covering of the surrounding plaza allows daylight to flood into the ovoid underground space of Calatrava's World Trade Center Transportation Hub, penetrating through all levels by means of glass-block floors to the train platform, approximately 70 feet below the street. At night the direction of light is reversed so that the structure is illuminated from the space underground like a lantern. The project itself, strange, captivating, enigmatic as it is, also radiates a rare aura of technical perfection, aesthetic rightness, and epic public monumentality.

Reinforcing the drama of the overall design is the presence of explicit physical movement: the structure's "wings" unfold on fine days in spring and summer, expressing further the sense of chthonic darkness mitigated by exposure to the greater world.

Certainly the enthusiastic reception of the theme of light relates to its symbolic role as a powerful vitalizing force. In a very schematic way this celebration of light, rather than the brute force of height, appeared as the most proper – and the most universal – representation of optimism.

In this sense Calatrava opted for an iconological repertory that describes timelessness and a cyclical, year-round process to emphasize the triumph of regeneration and revitalization rather than the memory of a single point in time that represents only catastrophe. Only on September 11 each year will the roof reach its maximum opening of 45 feet, bringing into the building a slice of sky and its light at an angle, commemorating the tragic events of that day in 2001.

above
Render

side
General ground plan

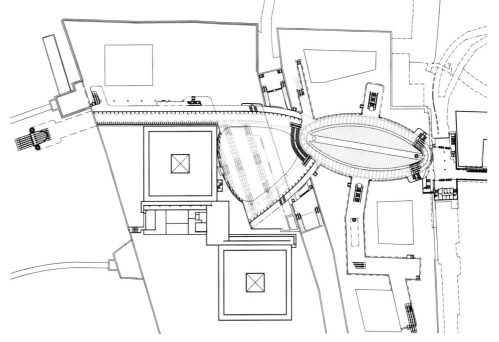

Tower (Fordham Spire)
Chicago, USA, 2005

Model of the tower

opposite page
Partial view of tower
and waterfront

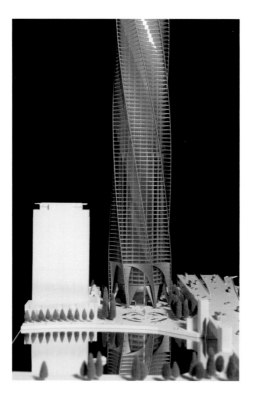

Rising to a height of 2,060 feet, this 115-story reinforced concrete tower featuring a steel and glass facade, will be the tallest in the United States. With a footprint at base of only 14,000 square feet, it is also one of the most slender. Crowned by a metal structural spike with integrated broadcast antennas, the tower serves several functions, combining a reception and restaurant area at ground level, hotel rooms on the lower levels and condominium residences on the upper levels. Adding to the building's uniqueness, each story is slightly rotated around the core of the building, so that it seems to turn in a spiral as it rises. The tower's circular plan provides all rooms with panoramic views of the city and lake. The space planning of the suites leaves a free zone around the perimeter of the floor plate, giving an open feeling to the interconnecting rooms and helping to maximize the views.

The project was commissioned for a very prominent site on the city's lakefront at Lake Shore Drive and North Water Street, near the meeting point of the Chicago River and Lake Michigan. Thanks to its twister-like profile, the tower when built will dominate the city's skyline.

Thought

A Story of Patient Research

An Interview with Santiago Calatrava

"I was born in Benimamet, a village near Valencia. In the neighbouring village there was an Arts and Crafts school, where my brother, because of my interest in drawing, enrolled me when I was barely eight years old. As seen from my present perspective, that was very interesting, because the people I was learning how to draw with were engravers, glass craftsmen, carvers; that is people who were still trained in the early 19th-century traditions. I, who by the way was one of the youngest, only attended that school for two years. I went no further than the charcoal pencil. […] I remember that after the drawing classes one could stay and attend history classes, where they would teach you that the column was composed of base, shaft and capital. […] Later, my parents enrolled me in a high school in Valencia – which in my view was a mistake. I left in the morning and returned home at night, with no time left to do anything else. Even today I believe that this period was a kind of error, because the logical thing would have been to continue that half-schooling system, drawing every day, and attending history classes afterwards. […] I find that for me to have gone to school in Valencia represented a break-up. In fact, instinctively, once I finished the pre-college course I decided to enrol in the Fine Arts School in Paris; and so there I was, in 1968. Not in May, but in June. […] I saw the sort of ruin Paris was reduced to. I came into contact with many people who had actively participated in the May revolution (I worked in a restaurant for some time) and thus I became aware of their disenchantment, their resignation. […] But, of course, I could not enrol in the Fine Arts school because, as a matter of fact, that School did not exist. The building had been destroyed. […] The most bizarre thing is that everybody wanted to leave the city. People never stopped organizing trips. […] Thus, I went back to Valencia and I enrolled in Arts and Crafts and in the Architecture school at the same time. For a year I followed both studies in parallel, until I left Arts and Crafts, where I attended evening classes, and I devoted myself entirely to architecture. […] The discipline I most worked on in school was

Projects. I would submit a number of drawings. I never made any extra efforts, except in this particular subject matter. I did quite well in it, too. […] In other words, I was a fairly good student. But, from the beginning Projects interested me. […] At that time I used to resort a great deal to the School Library. I gulped books down. I educated myself a great deal. […] I studied architecture with pleasure. Those studies made me mature, really, partially due to the fact that I was, to a great extent, self-taught. In those times, the School in Valencia was relatively unconsolidated – it did not have the tradition Madrid or Barcelona had – and most of the time is was closed down. Those years – 1969 to 1973 – were years of conflict. All of this led me, as I say, to a self-taught working system. Although the most decisive aspect to me was the chance to travel. I would use the summer months. I remember that I used to leave after the last exam, about June 28, and would return in November, just before the beginning of classes. Those were informal trips, carried out with the most unlikely means, and always on a minimum budget: a back-pack, a sleeping bag, and sandwiches. […] All of this is perhaps the most significant feature of my training as an architect. […] I intended to work and to continue studying outside Spain. I had good references at the Zurich Polytechnic, I had heard it was a good place to study engineering. If I had thought of studying something else, perhaps I would have gone somewhere else. But Switzerland has an outstanding tradition in engineering, so I went there. […] My way of doing things is very linear, in the sense that I am someone who can combine very few things, so when I started engineering I devoted myself exclusively to it, leaving architecture aside. I went back to studying mathematics, mechanics, hydraulics, and all those things. And in the summer, instead of taking trips, I would prepare the September exams. Those were studies drastically different from the studies in Spain. With few classroom mates, fantastic professors, etc […] I started to do rather scientific works, one of which, dealing with the foldability of structures, was useful to me later in preparing my doctorate. […] I worked a lot with models, studying kinetic problems. I was not an excessively brilliant student as far as the analysis of structures was concerned, but I was the most skilful in visualizing them, which was the part I was most interested in. […] My training was much more visual than that of my mates. I believe this was due, to some extent, to my previous architecture studies. I have a very photographic memory. Not everybody has it. […] My approach to architecture and engineering is, to a great extent, made up of images. My projects, even from the time I was in school, were and still are mainly formal, at a time when formalism was frowned upon. I believe this has to do with my first experiences, that is, had I not interrupted my studies in the Arts and Crafts School, I would have ended up a carver, or a model maker, something which is really inborn in me. All this took me to a peculiar training, which was not so much translated in reading treatise texts, classical or modern, as in visualizing, gathering images. […] Reading a book is something rather cold, whereas the contact with reality may tutor you on certain aspects in a very important manner. During the trips that I took I visited almost all that can be visited of the works of Le Corbusier in Europe, Alvar Aalto, Gio Ponti, Hans Scharoun. […] When I finished engineering I had to reeducate myself in architecture; in other words, I had to re-learn how to make plans and sections. […] Which was very helpful, as I discovered that the plan must be something orderly, plain, whereas the section may be complex, technical. […] I have heard it said (said because I have not read it) that in his *Treatise on Architecture*, Daniele Barbaro makes a series of remarks on beauty, on the meaning of construction, on the human attributes referred to in the Vitruvian doctrine: the firmitas, utilitas and venustas and, of particular interest to me, on the meaning of the plan and the section. To him, the plan gives order, and the section gives beauty. This is very interesting to me. The fact that beauty, Mother Nature, is read in the section makes you understand that all those mathematical outlines used in classical times related to proportion; […] a non architect cannot understand how different a plan is from a section. It is the section which synthesises the space.

As working tools, as controlling tools of the project, the plan and the section work very differently. The bringing up of a sense of beauty through the section seems to me very appropriate. In my work, the structural, tectonic device is most important. That is why I insist so much on the section. And for this reason the section plays such an important role in my work, and not so much the plan. Perhaps, even through self-limitation, I resort to very simple plans, as simple as possible. I don't remember ever having made complicated plans; moreover, in many cases – up until now, fortunately – plans have been more or less dictated by the project. […]

The scale is a very peculiar problem. And it is a problem that I discovered after finishing school. […] It is obvious that when one designs cutlery, you can touch it, you can put it in your mouth. […] The relation with cutlery is much greater than what you can have with an architectural work. Do you understand what I mean? The size of a sketch, whether for a piece of cutlery or for a project, is exactly the same. This is the only thing they have in common: formalism, to use a somewhat strong term. In common they have the formal impulse; their difference is the problem of scale. To give you an example: when I show in a lecture the slides of the Ernsting's project plan, people think that the folding doors are three or four meters in size, which is due to the protection parts placed at the entrances, located in the door's corners. Those poles seem to be sixty centimetres long, instead of the 2 meters forty centimetres their real size is. […] It is a transgression of the scale you never become aware of (I find, however, that this is not a bad thing…) Take the Seville bridge. There was no urban context. Surpassing the height of the Giralda (the tower of the Cathedral of the Giralda was the highest building in Seville) was not an issue. […] The Giralda and the bridge are never going to be seen together. The bridge is totally outside the city. If I had had to build the bridge in the middle of Seville, it would have been a different matter. The scale of the Barcelona bridge, on the contrary, is defined in relation to its surroundings. Context is very important in this case. This bridge could have been easily much too small for that very large

Wave, sculpture

space measuring hundreds of square meters. If I had not made the arches big and if the stairway and arches had not been a unity, the bridge would have become too small (and additionally, it would have collapsed). It would have been a great pity. It would have been like placing a small sculpture in the middle of a very big square. A disaster! Remember the figures of Christ and his mother in Michelangelo's *Pietà*? The mother is the right scale in a seated position. But if she stood up, she would be two meters twenty centimetres high! Do you understand what I mean? The relation proportion-size within a context is very important. Or, to add another example, take the new bridge in Merida that I am working on. We have proposed a two hundred-meter long arch, which is a grand architectural gesture, totally out of scale with the dimensions of the support on which it is based. This, I think, is one of the finest aspects of the project. It is like Mozart's Symphonia Concertante for viola and violin. One of the most monumental things in the history of music is the way in which the soloist instrument enters the first movement.

Mozart follows the melody in a linear fashion, and suddenly, as if from nowhere, the violin appears, which later will dominate the scene. [...] In the case of Merida the arch is out of scale. But this is not a bad thing, is it? Well, I hope not! [...] It goes against the context, it does not bow to it in a subordinate way. The easiest thing would have been to build one more Roman bridge.
[...]
The easiest thing to do is to empty a building and renovate it inside. To leave the facade on, even if it is very ugly. This is a way to avoid problems. People in this profession, architecture, tend to be complacent and take things as they are. What is it that you want? Potatoes? Here you are, potatoes! Instead of saying, well, let's give him a blue blossomed potato plant. Do you understand what I am trying to say? There are plenty of things an architect can invent. [...] For me, of course, it seems appropriate to invent a new object, to perform a technical feat. Sculpture has always interested me a great deal. Foldability and mobility are aspects that increasingly interest me. In the

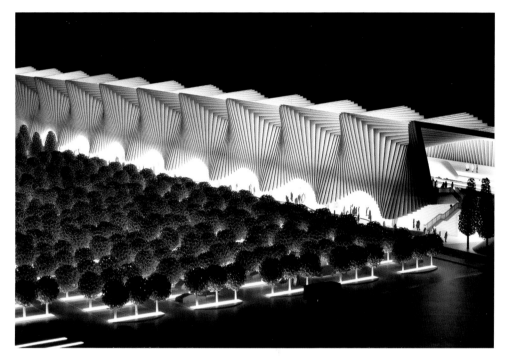

Model of the Reggio Emilia
train station

beginning I had to set up the office work. Now I have perhaps some more time and I can make machines or things like that. I am especially interested in the idea of a kinetic system applied to building. There is something I frequently repeat. It is almost commonplace already. It is the concept of force. [...] Look, in architecture as in mechanics, strength is equal to mass by acceleration. Mass is an abstract universal unit. Mobility is implicit in the concept of strength. A simple way of translating all of this is to say that forces are like crystallized movements. I am very much interested in that crystallized movement, and all the formal context this involves. Which has much to do with sculpture, with Rodin, Brancusi. [...] For example, a door, a window, or a mobile wall, are inventions already in existence and which, curiously, do not have an a priori space quality. Normally in our culture we almost always understand such mobile apparatus as flat apparatus, that is, with a vertically turning axis which allows for an opening. There are some interesting tests in space windows, such as in the case of Mackintosh, or certain things by Marcel

Duchamp, or in the Dutch Neoplasticists. [...] The actual fact of going overboard – such as in the case of the Ernsting's plant – is something relatively new in my work. That is, something which is a facade unit, becomes a sculptural unit, also as a facade, etc. Ultimately, the kinetic component is truly logical. It is like saying: if force is the result of mass by acceleration, let us make things move, balance, or whatever! Let's endow buildings with movement, beyond those elements that we all know: doors, windows, closets, canopies [...]. Let's attempt to make movement explicit and to introduce the dynamic aspect to other parts of the building. For architecture to move in new ways [...]. I personally find this highly stimulating [...]. From a theoretical viewpoint, the 19th century and its transition to the 20th century has always greatly interested me. Transitions from one century to another are usually very interesting. Oddly enough, in Spain at present, all attention has focused on 1992. This is sad because it is nothing more than a sort of a veil that conceals the real fact of the transition. This is why my

Study for a tower,
Serpentine Column

attitude – somewhat speculative – appears to me as more satisfactory than the attitude of whomever tries to establish his work immediately. I guess it also has to do with age. I am interested in breaking barriers, and creating a context more than doing what everyone else is doing. I see my work as more related to the future than the past. This is what all the little experiments I have carried out really mean[1]. do not willingly belong to any context, not even to the Swiss context. [...] My projects have a certain utopian, visionary character. [...] Avantgardes are necessarily created by young people. This does not mean that my work may be of interest from a critical architectural viewpoint or that I attain the sought-after result in my work. [...] There is a great deal of intellectual consumerism. An easily understood and quickly assimilated work may not be as innovative as it seems at first. This is why it is interesting to work in marginal contexts. The avantgarde, a concept that has, regrettably, now lost value, must be revived. [...]

At a certain moment, I devoted myself to the study of organic forms, with which my work has some similarities. This is the result of a clear choice and not so much with how to solve a given structural problem. I am increasingly tempted by simple forms, by minimizing [...]. My work is figurative rather than organizational, in the sense that I am interested in certain sculptural-anatomical relationships. Working with isostatic structures almost inevitably leads one to nature sketches. When a dog stands on his four legs, it constitutes an isostatic body. The load is divided by the number of legs; there are no reinforcements other than those supplied by the muscles. [...] On the other hand, I work a great deal on freehand sketches. I use squares and triangles very little, especially in these last years. Among other reasons because, at a certain point in time, I realized that drawing and architecture arc two different things. Architecture is a phenomenon in itself. It comes rather from the world of ideas directly applied onto the material being built. [...]

Graphics, as an intervening instrument, has now become a quasi Hindrance to me. Architecture is normally accomplished only through building materials. The plans and sections are just instruments for critical analysis […]. For this reason I decided to get away from drawing and to apply myself much more to an idea: the concept of space. And this not so much as the professor who wants to teach lessons, but as the student who wants to learn. It is as if someone who knows how to paint using his right hand, starts to draw using his left hand so as to give more thought to each stroke. […]

In my office there are many engineers and few draftsmen, as here the calculation portion is the main task, contrary to what is the case in other offices. […] The people that are useful to me as working tools are people with very little training, but who can use the Rotring quickly and who know to interpret a sketch. I use other people's hands for my own work. For that reason I prefer to hire a student rather than a well rounded architect, as the latter already has his own ideas and logically wishes to develop them, something which does not suit me, as project work is something tremendously personal. As opposed to what happens with people working on the final project, or during construction, these people require much less correction, as the generic parameters have already been given at a 1/100 scale. […] Even so, this is an office which is not very oriented toward financial criteria. In fact I believe that I have resisted because I am here, in Zurich, a place where fair fees are paid, and paid on time. Even so, I think that this office is too experimental. It demands a brutal effort. This is the reason why I work at home. In this manner I avoid having to take the tram and things like that. Is a lot more comfortable, and you can also work longer hours. […]

I am interested, to an almost excessive degree, in developing the concept of high technology concrete. Concrete is a material which has become a little displaced; in other words, it is a material out of fashion, and to me it is probably the most noble construction material there is, in the sense that it adapts perfectly to any needs.
[…]

From a perspective of the future, I am sure that together with steel, concrete shall become the great material of the 21st century. […] My interest is centred in introducing a new vocabulary, of soft forms, of a surrealist character, somewhat in tune with the spirit of the times (even though I do not much believe in my time) […]; despite the fact that they are very much based on technical know-how, I do not believe that my works are an anthem to techniques. […]

There is an obvious interest by some cultural sectors in purchasing architectural drawings. This is because everybody knows that drawings – or at any rate, what is understood as drawings nowadays – are going to disappear (there are people which are obsessively engaged in purchasing architectural drawings). It is like buying hand-carved furniture. Hand carving has become obsolete.

"Conversaciones con Richard Levene y Fernando Marquez, Zürich, Febrero 1989", in *Santiago Calatrava 1983-93*, catalogue for the exhibit, Madrid: El Croquis, 1993, pp. 10-16.

Photographers

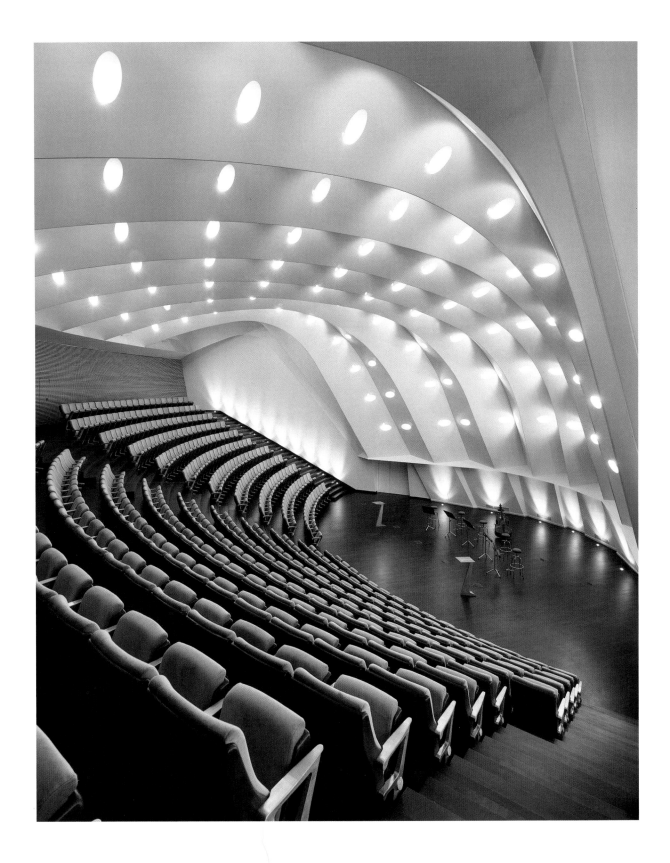

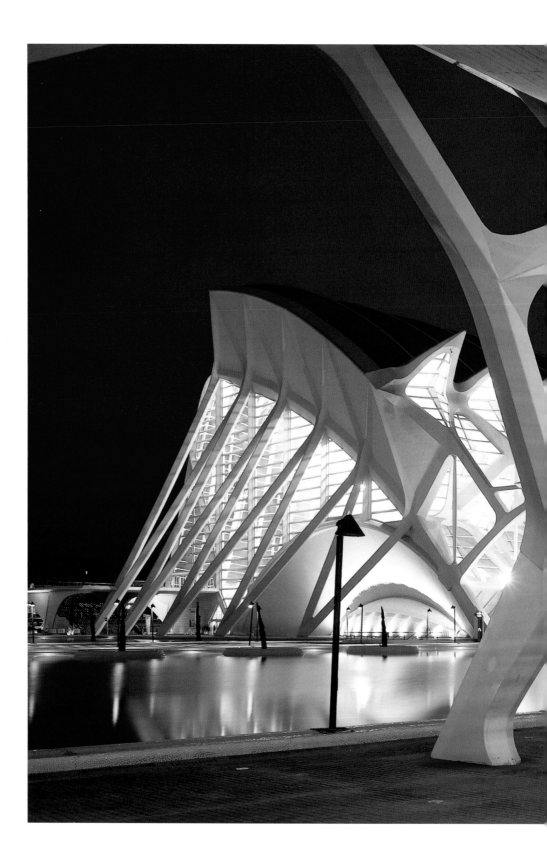

Critique

Thoughts on the Poetic of Motion

Michael Levin
A workshop of ideas, shapes and structures

Santiago Calatrava is a universal designer engaged in a number of fields: architecture, engineering, design, and art. His work in all areas marries combines structure and movement, creating a unique synthesis which imbues forms with elements of surprise and poetry.

From the beginning of his career (after graduating in 1981), Calatrava foreshadowed a trend that characterized the trend characterizsing the art world of the late 20th century, consisting in of blurred boundaries between various art forms. Many of today's artists no longer care to be defined as strictly painters, sculptors or designers, seeing their field of occupation as interdisciplinary or as being on the seam between the various professions.

Interestingly, Calatrava, whose fame to date has focused until now has been known mainly on for his architectural work, views art as an inspiration sees in art a stimulus for his oeuvre at large. His preoccupation with art over the years finds expression in the astounding number of drawings and sculptures he has created to date. In the course of the last two decades, more than 65,000 drawings have been accumulated in his archive. Some of the forms and subjects initially investigated in his the drawings were ill later be developed into sculptures, which in turn may eventually may have served serve as the inspiration for bridges, railway stations, airports, museums – or even dining room tables.

Calatrava indeed emphasizses that his lexicon of forms does not derive from engineering or architecture but, rather, from ideas that were sown in the drawings and sometimes germinated in the sculptures. Over the years, along with designing bridges and railway stations, Calatrava has created more than a hundred sculptures as well as sketches for many others, which have not yet been realiszed. Until now he has rarely displayed his artwork.

The drawings and sculptures should be contemplated as works of art in their own right. At the same time, being germinal stages in Calatrava's creative process, they also constitute a laboratory or seedbed for the development of an overall concept, a means of quickening thought and crystallizsing a contemporary, individual Ggestalt of forms. This laboratory generates a reservoir of ideas that emanate from a dialogue an interaction with nature and with forms manifested in art and architecture throughout history. Here memories from the past intermesh with visions for the world of the future – a synthesis of engineering, mathematics, design per se, and structures answering that respond to specific functional needs.

Nonetheless, Calatrava does not hesitate to interrelate relate, simultaneously at times concurrently, withto diverse artists and styles that range from – to Rodin to, Degas and Max Bill and from; to Classicism and, Gothicism to and Constructivism. But he approaches the history of art as a quarry to be mined in the quest for innovative form and content. He aspires to fathom comprehend the essence of the work that which interests him and, to seek answers to the questions it prompts.

For Calatrava, then, the process of design begins with the creation of abstract forms. Form derives from mathematical research, from experiments in movement and from the integration of movement into structure, but never from aspiring to the ultimate functional objective. The vast number of his drawings attests to the intensity with which Calatrava forges his singular world of forms; and it serves him in all fields, from art to engineering.

The advantage of an accumulating, expanding and modifying repository of forms lies in its being an inexhaustible and crystallizsed source, which has already undergone an initial process of development and experimentation. The artist has recourse to this repository whenever he is faced with a task calling for requiring a concrete solution; the final objective guides his choice from among the existing images and ideas, and only at this stage do considerations of statics, gravitation and function enter the picture as elements in the project's work's evolution.

Movement constitutes a central theme also in Calatrava's architectural oeuvre. His preoccupation with movement is evident from the earliest stages of his career and finds expression in all media. As a young architect, he joined the team Fabio Reinhart and Bruno Reichlin team in redesigning the Ernsting Warehouse in, Coesfeld, Germany (1983-84). The building's image was dramatically transformed by covering the facades with corrugated aluminium, creating a sense of movement as a result of the play of light and shade on the rippled wall surfaces, enhanced by the eye's back-and-forth movement along with the building's body. The dynamic quality is further enhanced by the mechanical opening and closing of the folding doors. Calatrava's design turned their upward/downward movement from a functional solution to a kinetic sculpture: when the doors rise, the folds produce an intriguing cantilevered roof effect.

Here again, architecture prefigured art, and the concept of the changing form, composed of densely spaced parallel strips, was later developed in sculptures. The idea first formulated in the warehouse doors evolved into the model for a vertical sculpture, where the movement is only implied. Later (1993) he would conceive a more complex composition in wood, with the strips latticed in two versions – sparsely in one, densely in the other. The next variation of the ribs is seen evident in the sculpture *Waves* (1994), where the form serves no functional purpose, its source of inspiration and movement originating being found in Nnature rather than in the world of mechanics. Measuring 1.50 by 5 metres, this work comprises a sheet of corrugated metal rippling in asymmetrical hyperbolic and parabolic motion that creates a sense of rolling waves and inspires invites contemplation. The pleasure derived from prolonged viewing of this sculpture is much like that of gazing at the sea from the deck of a ship. There is something hypnotic, tranquil and timeless about the sea's constant movement, and Calatrava masterfully conveys this sensation in the sculpture. Its soft movement rocks the viewer into a dreamlike state, an effect also attained in s also evoked, for example, by his bird sculptures, for example, suggesting gliding flight.

side
Suspended Object
or Discerning Eye, sculpture

below
Aegean cycle sculpture

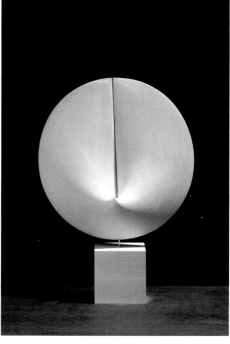

Calatrava makes powerful use of arrested movement in his bridge designs, as in the Bach de Roda Bridge, in Barcelona (1984-87), and the Alamillo Bridgein, Seville (1987-92). We find aArrested movement also characterises in the sculpture *Eye II*, a sculpture that the shape of which resembles a the human eye. The hollow "eyeball" rests on strings, stretched between the two ends of the crescent, describing the lower part of an eye, as depicted in a related drawing. In another drawing, a similar crescent is formed by the extended arms of a figure playing with a yo-yo. Calatrava's enchantment with the eye motif is evinced in additional sketches illustrating showing a central, variously sized sphere

supported by adjoining shapes, from the eye-like ellipse and central sphere to the huge spherical form whose scale is defined by diminutive human figures. Here the sphere is sustained by wire linked to the vertical rectangles on either side. In yet another drawing a large disk hovers slightly above a semi-circular base and is held in place by wires attached to its sides. A variation of this motif is found in a drawing of a large circle resting on a small base. Calatrava has contrived to create a synthesis of his engagement with nature, form and art through the ages, as well as with 20th-century sculpture and architecture. His exhilarating forms have been arrived at were attained through a rare combination of poetry

Manrique pedestrian bridge, Murcia

opposite page
Alamillo Bridge, Seville

and oneiric elements dream paired with with an engineering expertise in which mathematical and static calculations do not constitute a separate aspect of the work but are organically integrated into its overall concept. The well-spring of ideas and forms summed glimpsed in this book arouses stirs admiration for Calatrava's the sheer creativity of Calatrava, combined with the anticipation for of their sequel in his drawings, sculptures and structures yet to be born.

M. Levin, *Santiago Calatrava. Art Works*, Basel: Birkhäuser, 2003, pp. 7-9.

Anthony Tischhausser

Excerpts from "Aspects of Movement in the Work of Santiago Calatrava"

"In understanding mechanical analysis, we see that the forces are made up of two components: mass and the acceleration of mass. A force is the result of the product of a mass and its acceleration. Mass is the universal constant of each body; acceleration is variable. In this simple formula, it seems to me that acceleration is part of a kinematic world; 'kinematic' implies a variable for movement, and in fact acceleration takes place in space and time. So within
a force, time is also variable, since forces present mass at a universal constant. Time thus appears to be the result of acceleration. Forces are not so permanent. I could almost say that forces are like crystallized movement. Forces are events that will only take place in certain conditions of time. They do not happen because – like ice – they are crystallized. But when released, they will produce movement through space."
Santiago Calatrava

Such mechanical implications are not generally associated with architecture, and mechanics is rarely recognized as a basis for architectural design. For Calatrava, however, mechanics is always a source of inspiration, and represents an entire field of invention. Static or dynamic, it is not only the transition between one type of movement and another, but also between one material and another.
"My approach to design begins with the creation of toys and games that can give plastic expression to the principles of statics," Calatrava has said. Calatrava the engineer experiments with the laws of statics. But it is equally fascinating to consider mechanics in terms of movement and dynamics, and this inevitable movement is poetically transposed by Calatrava the artist: "The images of forces at work are a demonstration of forces at work. They may even reveal the ideas behind my architecture more effectively than any finished building or construction." In the architecture of Santiago Calatrava, movement is a major theme and can be understood on many levels. Entire components of Calatrava's buildings are bought into motion, transforming one space into another and one function into another. Indeed, his buildings take function beyond mere function, to become statements on the quality of space – they become "superfunctional." […]
It is movement that leads us to associate an apparent lightness with Calatrava's architecture. This quality can be traced back to an early interest in temporary folding structures. Erecting and taking down a primitive shelter such as a tent or market stand is based on movement. The image of a sequence of elements slotted together to form and define spaces is reminiscent of analyses of motion such as those by Eadweard Muybridge. The beauty in such processes is captured by Calatrava in an analogy that was to head his academic explorations, and which is illustrated by the image of a staccato-like unfolding of a bud into a blossom and the accompanying remark: "Nature is mother and teacher." […]
The shapes and forms applied and evolved by Calatrava always appear moulded and crafted, which is unusual considering both the size of the spaces he often creates and the nature of the elements employed. Calatrava always aims to maintain a sense of flow in the structural members. This is in marked contrast to the current trend for emphasizing the lifeless "warehouse effect," not only in terms of spatial feeling and

opposite page
Campo Volantin Bridge, Bilbao

117

temporality of structure (although such structures are most often designed for long-term use) but in the bland engineering aesthetic of off-the-shelf tubes welded together to form a structure. Calatrava goes beyond such abstract rationale; once the approach is established, the actual work really begins with the form-giving process – with the architecture. Architecture evolves through structure; it is not in itself structure. It is this quality that makes Calatrava's architecture and spatial identity so incredibly popular. "No building is just a building; a building determines the image of a city," he has said.

The art of architecture is the creation of harmony in tension: the tension of a structure in relation to its setting; the tension between form and construction. That is the real challenge. Such a carefully crafted industrial process contrasts with current fads in building and with the cultural paucity of the technical shed, no matter how ingeniously it may be conceived. Calatrava the master builder challenges the industrial process by bringing movement into the very process of manufacture. Individual static elements are used to imply movement which is then explicitly brought about by assembling elements to form the basis of unfolding dynamic spaces. Movement is a feeling for forces expressed and applied in Calatrava's individual way. "The centre of gravity is not where you would expect it, but consciously somewhere else." This apparent lack of inherent equilibrium is the basis for the feeling of movement in Calatrava's work.

Santiago Calatrava, Architectural Monographs , n. 46 , London: Academy Editions, 1996.

Bibliography

Santiago Calatrava, catalogue for the exhibit, Galerie Jamileh Weber, Weinfelden: Wolfau-Druck/Rudolf Mühlemann, 1986.

W. Blaser, *Santiago Calatrava Ingenieur-Architektur*, Basel: Birkhäuser, 1987.

R.C. Levene, F. Márquez Cecilia, *Santiago Calatrava 1983/1989*, Madrid: El Croquis, 1989.

M. McQuaid, *Santiago Calatrava. Structure and Expression*, catalogue for the exhibit, New York: Museum of Modern Art, 1992.

K. Frampton, A.C. Webster, A. Tischhauser, *Santiago Calatrava. Bridges*, Zurich: Birkhäuser, 1993.

A. Tzonis, L. Lefaivre, *Movement, Structure and the Work of Santiago Calatrava*, Basel: Birkhäuser, 1995.

M. Zardini, *Santiago Calatrava. Secret Sketchbook*, Milan: Federico Motta Editore, 1995.

A. Tischhauser, S. von Moos, *Santiago Calatrava. Public Buildings*, Basel: Birkhäuser, 1998.

M. Blanco, *Santiago Calatrava*, catalogue for the exhibit, Valencia: Generalitat Valenciana, 1999.

A. Tzonis, *Santiago Calatrava. The Poetics of Movement*, New York: Universe Publishing, 1999.

Santiago Calatrava. Sculptures and Drawings Escultures y Dibuixos, catalogue for the exhibit, IVAM Centre Julio Gonzales, Valencia: Aldeasa/IVAM 2001.

A. Tzonis, *Santiago Calatrava. Creative Process Fundamentals*, Basel: Birkhäuser, 2001.

A. Tzonis, L. Lefaivre, *Santiago Calatrava. Sketchbooks*, Basel: Birkhäuser, 2001.

C.L. Kausel, A. Pendleton-Jullian, *Santiago Calatrava. Conversations with Students*, Princeton: Princeton Architectural Press, 2002.

L. Lefaivre, *Santiago Calatrava Wie ein Vogel / Like a Bird*, catalogue for the exhibit, Genève-Milan: Skira, 2003.

M. Levin, *Santiago Calatrava Artworks*, Basel: Birkhäuser, 2003.

S. Calatrava, *Calatrava Alpine Bridges*, Weinfelden: Wolfau-Druck, 2004.

A. Tzonis, *Santiago Calatrava. The Complete Works*, New York: Rizzoli, 2004.

A. Tzonis, R. Caso Donadei, *Santiago Calatrava. The Bridges*, New York: Rizzoli, 2005.

A. Tzonis, *Santiago Calatrava, The Athens Olympics*, New York: Rizzoli, 2005.